134

Sea Otters

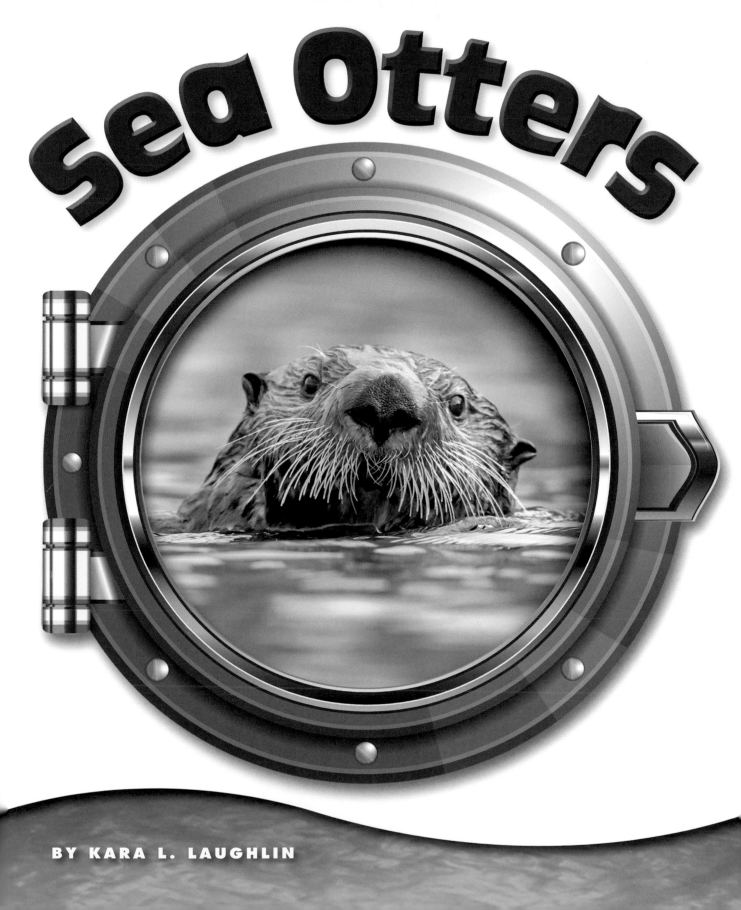

BY KARA L. LAUGHLIN

The Child's World®
childsworld.com

Published by The Child's World®
1980 Lookout Drive • Mankato, MN 56003-1705
800-599-READ • www.childsworld.com

DESIGN ELEMENTS
© creatOR76/Shutterstock.com: porthole
© keren-seg/Shutterstock.com: water

PHOTO CREDITS
© 44kmos/Shutterstock.com: 18-19; David Litman/Shutterstock.com: 12-13; Focus no.5/Shutterstock.com: 15; KGrif/Shutterstock.com: 8-9; Menno Schaefer/Shutterstock.com: cover, 1, 6-7, 14; neelsky/Shutterstock.com: 20-21; Ryan M. Bolton/Shutterstock.com: 5; Terence/Shutterstock.com: 17; Wildnerdpix/Shutterstock.com: 11

ISBN: 9781503816893
LCCN: 2016945598

Printed in the United States of America
PA02326

NOTE FOR PARENTS AND TEACHERS

The Child's World® helps early readers develop their informational-reading skills by providing easy-to-read books that fascinate them and hold their interest. Encourage new readers by following these simple ideas:

BEFORE READING
- Page briefly through the book. Discuss the photos. What does the reader think he or she will learn in this book? Let the child ask questions.
- Look at the glossary together. Discuss the words.

READ THE BOOK
- Now read the book together, or let the child read the book independently.

AFTER READING
- Urge the child to think more. Ask questions such as, "What things are different among the animals shown in this book?"

Contents

Floating and Furry

What are those cute animals floating in the water? They are sea otters.

Sea otters are **mammals**. They have fur. They breathe air.

4

Water Bodies

Sea otters have long bodies. They are good swimmers. Their back feet are **webbed**. A flat tail helps them steer.

Help for Kelp

Some sea otters live in **kelp forests**.
Kelp forests are important places.
Many kinds of animals live there.

Did you know?

Kelp can grow up to 175 feet (53 meters) high.

Sea otters keep kelp forests healthy.
They eat animals that kill kelp.

Sea Otter Families

Male sea otters are called **boars**. Female sea otters are called **sows**. A baby sea otter is called a **pup**. Sea otters gather in groups called **rafts**.

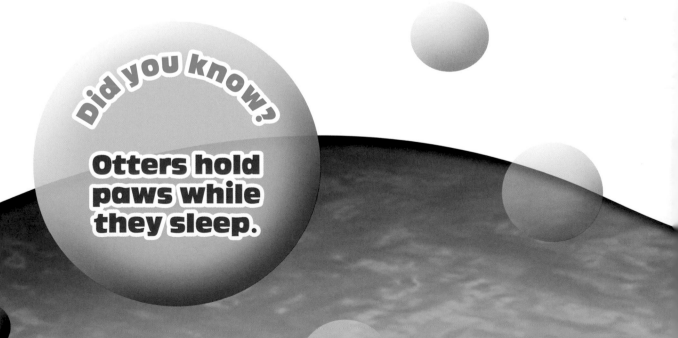

Did you know?

Otters hold paws while they sleep.

Sows hold pups on their chests. They give them milk. Sows must leave their pups to hunt. The pups are okay. Their fur makes them float.

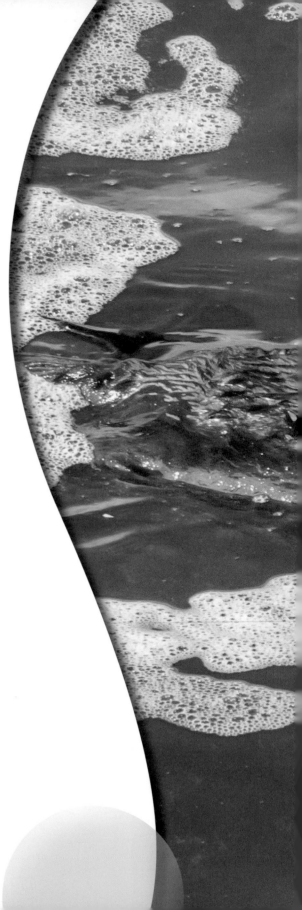

Did you know?

Sea otter sows like to clean and fluff their pups' fur.

Food

Sea otters eat foods from the ocean floor. Their **whiskers** help them feel around when the sea is dark.

Sea otters eat crabs, clams, and other animals with shells.

Did you know?

Sea otters also eat some kinds of fish.

Using Tools

Sea otters sometimes use rocks to break open the shells. Sea otters float on their backs while they eat.

Did you know?

Sea otters have 32 teeth. Most of them are flat for chewing.

Did you know?

There were once
fewer than 2,000
sea otters left
in the world.

Help for Sea Otters

At one time, sea otters were almost gone. People hunted them for fur. Oil spills killed many sea otters. Now there are laws to keep sea otters safe.

Sea otters are more than just cute. They are important animals in the sea.

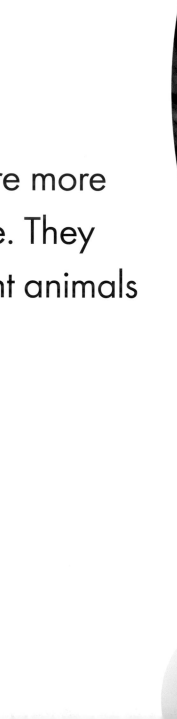

Did you know?

Sea otters
live for about
15 years.

GLOSSARY

boar (BOR): A male sea otter is called a boar.

kelp forest (KELP FOR-est): Kelp is seaweed that grows very tall. When a lot of kelp is in one area, it is called a kelp forest.

mammal (MAM-mull): A mammal is an animal that is warm-blooded. Mammal mothers feed their babies milk from their bodies. Sea otters and people are mammals.

pup (PUP): A baby sea otter is called a pup.

raft (RAFT): A group of sea otters is called a raft.

sow (SOW): A female sea otter is called a sow.

webbed (WEBD): Webbed is having skin that stretches between an animal's toes. Sea otters have webbed feet.

whiskers (WISS-kurz): Whiskers are long, stiff hairs near an animal's mouth. Whiskers help animals feel their way around.

TO LEARN MORE

On the Web

Visit our Web page for
lots of links about sea otters:
www.childsworld.com/links

Note to parents, teachers, and librarians:
We routinely verify our Web links to make
sure they are safe, active sites—
so encourage your readers
to check them out!

In the Library

Eszterhas, Suzi. *Sea Otter Rescue*. Toronto, Ontario:
Owlkids Books, 2016.

Marsh, Laura. *Sea Otters*. Washington, DC:
National Geographic, 2014.

Schuh, Mari. *Sea Otters*. Minneapolis, MN:
Bullfrog Books, 2016.

INDEX

About the Author

Kara L. Laughlin is an artist and writer who lives in Virginia with her husband, three kids, two guinea pigs, and a dog. She is the author of two dozen nonfiction books for kids.